THE ESSENTIAL
LATE ROMANTIC
COLLECTION
FOR SOLO PIANO

CHESTER MUSIC
part of The Music Sales Group

London / New York / Paris / Sydney / Copenhagen / Berlin / Madrid / Tokyo

Published by
Chester Music Limited,
8/9 Frith Street, London, W1D 3JB, England.

Exclusive distributors:
Music Sales Limited,
Distribution Centre, Newmarket Road, Bury St Edmunds,
Suffolk, IP33 3YB, England.

Music Sales Pty Limited,
120 Rothschild Avenue, Rosebery,
NSW 2018, Australia.

Order No. CH70609
ISBN 1-84609-228-0
This book © Copyright 2006 by Chester Music Limited.

Arranging and engraving supplied by Camden Music.

Printed in the EU.

www.musicsales.com

Your Guarantee of Quality:
As publishers, we strive to produce every book
to the highest commercial standards.

The music has been freshly engraved. Particular care has been
given to specifying acid-free, neutral-sized paper made from pulps
which have not been elemental chlorine bleached.

This pulp is from farmed sustainable forests
and was produced with special regard for the environment.

Throughout, the printing and binding have been planned to ensure a sturdy,
attractive publication which should give years of enjoyment.

If your copy fails to meet our high standards, please inform us
and we will gladly replace it.

LATE ROMANTICISM

In 1853, the German composer, Robert Schumann, wrote in his diary: 'visit from Brahms, a genius'. Schumann went on to describe Brahms as music's long-awaited saviour, recognising in the work of his younger friend a perfect synthesis of romantic and classical styles: the music was as passionate as it was controlled, as lyrical as it was disciplined.

The late romantic period was an era of individualism and visionary endeavour. If Brahms's music represents a particular tendency of late romanticism—the attempt to try to unify romantic and classical styles—other composers tried to build on the foundation of early romanticism in less measured ways: in Wagner's later operas, a titanic dramatic vision is underpinned by harmony and orchestration of astonishing richness and grandeur. The Austrian symphonist, Anton Bruckner (Brahms's great rival in 1880s Vienna) tried to mirror Wagner's sense of visionary breadth and romantic warmth in his colossal symphonies. In the same city, Johann Strauss II (a friend of both Brahms and Wagner) brought the Viennese waltz to a new level of suavity and elegance.

The growth of nationalism throughout the 19th century had many different musical repercussions. In Italy, the expressive force and dramatic immediacy of Verdi's operas—particularly his stirring use of choruses—made an overwhelming impact on their first audiences. For Italians, Verdi's name became a potent political symbol as Italy headed inexorably towards unification. Meanwhile the Czech composer, Antonin Dvořák attempted to fuse the characteristics of Bohemian folk music with his own expertly crafted orchestral style. His famous *New World Symphony* was composed in 1893 during his period as a professor of composition in New York. Some of its melodies demonstrate Dvořák's enlightened interest in black-American popular styles. In Norway, Edvard Grieg, attempted to render the distinctive idioms of indigenous Norwegian music in a distinctively lush, late romantic style influenced by Liszt and Wagner.

In Russia, the operas of Rimsky-Korsakov combine elements of Russian folk music and post-Wagnerian harmony blended together in a richly fantastical orchestral style. No less impressive an orchestrator was Rimsky-Korsakov's compatriot, Tchaikovsky. Although his music was an eclectic mix of Russian, French and German influences, Tchaikovsky managed to forge a distinctive style that is at once elegant, colourful, melodious and deeply expressive. His symphonies, ballets, concertos and operas have proved to be enduringly and universally popular. The younger composer, Skryabin, was initially an imitator of Chopin but his particular genius for complex harmony led him in an increasingly mystical direction. This led not only to his fabulously sensuous later music, but also to his notoriously barmy declaration in 1905: 'Generally speaking, I am God'.

At the turn of the 20th century, a younger generation of composers began to take interesting new directions. The great Jewish-Austrian composer, Gustav Mahler, embarked on a series of colossal symphonies, influenced in part by Bruckner but imbued with a new psychological intensity (Mahler was a contemporary of Sigmund Freud, another Jew living in Vienna in the 1900s, and went to him for psychoanalysis). Mahler's works are remarkable both for their scale and the complexity of their orchestration, relying as much on subtle combinations of instruments as on huge orchestral effects.

In England, Elgar began the 20th-century renaissance of British music. Influenced as much by European music as by English forbears like Parry, Elgar managed to create his own richly melodic style, equally at home writing exquisite salon music, such as *Chanson de Matin* and *Salut d'Amour*, as he was writing monumental oratorios, symphonies or concertos.

In an era of enormous works, the French composer, Gabriel Fauré proved himself a master of intimacy and charm, writing beautifully original piano pieces, chamber music and songs. His hugely popular Requiem is most striking in its refusal to set the text in the usual melodramatic fashion, but rather in an atmosphere of meditative reflection.

Fauré's younger contemporaries, Satie and Debussy began to take a brave new direction towards impressionism. Satie was one of music's great eccentrics and his early piano pieces, such as the famous *Gymnopédies* attempted to evoke the atmosphere of ancient Greece in a ritualistic style that is both simple and sophisticated. Debussy, on the other hand, was a composer of much broader scope. His whole career was a reaction to the cult of Wagnerism (which seized France in the late 19th century) and his early works show the influence of Grieg. At the turn of the 20th century, he began to forge a deeply original style in his piano music as well as the opera *Pelléas et Mélisande* and his orchestral masterpiece, *La Mer*. Like his contemporaries, the painters Van Gogh and Cézanne, Debussy's music had a profound impact on the younger generation. Ravel, Bartók and Stravinsky all acknowledged his influence as they pushed on towards modernism.

Several of Debussy's piano pieces (most famously his *Golliwogg's Cake-walk*) make reference to the emerging syncopated style of black-American popular music. Scott Joplin, the finest composer of ragtime, composed his *Maple Leaf Rag* in 1899. It rapidly sold more sheet-music copies than any other score in history. Sadly, Joplin (who had a very unfavourable agreement with his publisher) failed to capitalise on his remarkable commercial achievement. He went on to compose many beautiful piano rags but he died in poverty in 1917.

LATE ROMANTIC COMPOSERS

Isaac Manuel Francisco Albéniz (1860–1909) was a Spanish pianist and composer of remarkable gifts. He gave his first public performance in Barcelona at the age of four and eight years later, he stowed away on a ship bound for America. He toured the USA as a performing pianist, earning enough money to fund his return to Europe where he took piano lessons with the aged Liszt in the 1880s. Later, he received composition lessons from the progressive French composers, d'Indy and Dukas in Paris.

Albéniz' style amalgamates the idioms of Spanish folk music with the sophistication of late romantic piano technique. His style became increasingly impressionistic and his masterpiece *Iberia* had a deep influence on the piano works of his friends, Debussy and Ravel.

Johannes Brahms (1833–1897) was born in Hamburg, the son of a freelance double-bass player. His family were not wealthy and Johannes' precocious gifts as a pianist were put to practical use playing in taverns and dance halls. However, his talents were quickly recognised. At the age of 22, the famous violinist Joachim was so impressed by Brahms that he took him to meet Schumann who declared him to be a genius on the spot. Brahms lived most of his mature life in Vienna where his compositions were increasingly acclaimed.

Brahms was one of the greatest composers of the romantic era. His music is deeply lyrical and passionate while maintaining a tightly controlled sense of form and balance. His infallible technique as a composer was underpinned by his profound knowledge of, and admiration for, baroque and classical music. He sometimes used works by Bach or Beethoven as models when undertaking new compositional projects. Brahms' work has maintained its classic status since his lifetime. His output consists of almost nothing but masterpieces. He composed orchestral, choral and chamber works, songs and piano music.

Max Bruch (1838–1920) travelled widely throughout his career as a conductor in various German cities (although he conducted in Liverpool for a period) and ended his career as professor of composition at the Berlin Academy. Most of his career was lived in the shadow of his greater contemporary, Brahms.

Bruch was very conservative in outlook and resisted the innovations of Liszt and Wagner, preferring a simpler harmonic style influenced by Mendelssohn. He loved folksong and many of his works use it as a melodic source. His famous first violin concerto of 1868 brought him early success, and has tended to overshadow his 100 other published works.

Anton Bruckner (1824–1896) came from a humble rural background and, throughout a lifetime of rigorous self-application, became one of Austria's leading composers.

Bruckner's early years were spent as a school teacher and organist. In his spare time he pursued a gruelling course of harmony and counterpoint studies. It was not until he was 41 years old that he embarked on his first symphony.

From then on, there was no restraining him. A series of titanic symphonies and religious works followed. In them, Bruckner demonstrated a deep understanding of the Viennese classics (his favourite composer was Mozart) combined with a desire to match the work of his hero Wagner in terms of scale and daring.

A devout roman catholic, Bruckner saw his work in vocational terms. However, he was plagued with constant self-doubts and most of his works underwent constant rewriting. He was, nevertheless, one of the most original composers of the late 19th century.

Samuel Coleridge-Taylor (1875–1912) was England's first successful black composer. Born in Croydon, the son of a doctor from Sierra Leone, he studied composition at the Royal College of Music. In 1898, while still a student, the Gloucester Festival—on the recommendation of Elgar—commissioned his *Romance In A Minor* for orchestra. However, it was the following year that Coleridge-Taylor sprang to prominence after the first performance of his highly popular cantata, *Hiawatha's Wedding Feast.*

Coleridge-Taylor was a talented conductor, much in demand in the USA where he made three tours and was known in New York as 'the black Mahler'. He was composition professor at Trinity College of Music and later at the Guildhall School of Music and Drama. Tragically, he died at the age of 37.

Claude Debussy (1862–1918) was one France's greatest composers and a pioneer of modernism. He studied at the Paris Conservatoire where he decided to embark on a career as a composer instead of becoming a concert pianist. In 1884 he won the famous Prix de Rome.

Debussy's first masterpiece was the orchestral piece *Prélude à l'Après-midi d'un Faune* of 1894, a piece of wonderful delicacy, seductively orchestrated.

He became internationally famous with his opera *Pelléas et Mélisande* in 1902. Thereafter, he embarked on a series of groundbreaking works for piano including *Images*, two books of Preludes and the late Etudes. His magnificent orchestral works, *Nocturnes* of 1897–1899 and *La Mer* (completed in Eastbourne in 1905) are among the most original works in the orchestral repertoire. His late ballet *Jeux* is thought by some to be his greatest masterpiece.

Antonin Dvořák (1841–1904) was the son of a Czech innkeeper. He established an early reputation in Prague with his early symphonies and chamber music, but it was not until Brahms recommended him to his publisher in 1875 that Dvořák achieved international celebrity with his first set of Slavonic Dances.

At the height of his fame, Dvořák took up a professorship in New York in 1892, during which time he composed his ninth symphony ('From the New World') and the 'American' string quartet. During his final years in Prague, he wrote a string of operas including the famous *Rusalka* (1900).

Dvořák's music was a powerful combination of Czech nationalistic elements with a sophisticated romantic style, influenced by Liszt, Wagner and later Brahms. His attractive and deeply felt music has been widely popular since his lifetime.

Edward Elgar (1857–1934) was born near Worcester, the son of a piano tuner. He was largely self-taught and spent the first 40 years of his career in provincial obscurity despite the local success of his impressive early choral pieces. However, in 1899, the premiere of his *'Enigma' Variations* for orchestra catapulted Elgar to international fame. He went on to compose the work he himself regarded as his masterpiece, *The Dream of Gerontius*. During this prolific period he wrote all his major orchestral works including two magnificent symphonies and two famous concertos. After the death of his wife in 1920, Elgar composed relatively little.

Elgar's music, though influenced by a number of romantic European composers from Wagner to Gounod, is nevertheless so characteristic that it has earned its own adjective 'Elgarian'. His was a curiously English genius. His bluff military bearing masked a deeply sensitive, often insecure character and his superb orchestral technique combines in his greatest works with depth of feeling, infallible harmonic control and an unsurpassed gift for melody.

Gabriel Fauré (1845–1924) trained as a church musician but it was not until he attended piano classes with the composer Saint-Saëns that he decided to embark on a compositional career.

Fauré was one of very few composers of his era to escape the overpowering influence of Wagner's music. For most of his career, he concentrated on composing chamber music, piano pieces and songs of the highest quality. He also wrote a large number of choral works, most notably the restrained and lyrical Requiem.

In some respects, Fauré's understated style is a reaction to all the overblown mannerisms of late romanticism. His was a harmonically subtle approach with transparent textures, a feeling for elegant melody and an ability to synthesise the musical language of his age into a personal style full of distinctly French charm. This is not however to deny the force and passion of many of his chamber works and songs which in some respects are comparable with Brahms in terms of quality of imagination and emotional range. His late works, including his opera *Penelope* are masterpieces of a peculiarly sparse and self-disciplined kind.

Edvard Grieg (1843–1907) was born in Bergen, Norway and was the first major composer to come from Scandinavia. Early in his career, he tried to compose a symphony but the experiment was not a happy one. Thereafter he turned his attention to miniatures: piano pieces and songs of such freshness and directness that they won much acclaim. Apart from his superb early piano concerto, three sonatas and a fine string quartet in G minor, his only large-scale work is the famous incidental music to Ibsen's *Peer Gynt*.

Grieg's style is highly individual. Although he rarely quoted folksongs, his music seems to breathe the character of his nation's music. The harmonic daring and lyricism of his music are as striking today as when they were first written.

Scott Joplin (1867–1917) was born in Texas, the son of a former slave. In the 1880s, he travelled the midwest as an itinerant musician and in the 1890s published his earliest ragtime pieces for piano, among them the *Maple Leaf Rag* which became a huge overnight success. Joplin's lifelong ambition was to see ragtime elevated to the status of an art form. The most challenging project of his career was his ragtime opera, *Treemoshina*. Sadly, his plans never reached fruition and *Treemoshina* remained unstaged until 1976 when it received a posthumous Pulitzer Prize. Joplin died of syphilis the day that the USA entered the first world war.

Scott Joplin's piano works are expertly written, often displaying lyrical, even nostalgic qualities.

Edward Macdowell (1860–1908) was born into a cultured American family who decided that young Edward's unusual gifts needed European cultivation. Consequently, he travelled to Europe in 1876 to develop his musical training.

Returning to Boston in 1888, Macdowell embarked on the composition of many delightful piano pieces, which he often performed in public. When Columbia University appointed him their first composition professor in 1896, he was described as 'the greatest musical genius America has produced'. Sadly, Macdowell found his teaching duties too gruelling and he suffered a mental breakdown which led to the insanity of his final years.

Gustav Mahler (1860–1911) was one of the greatest composers of his generation. His ten symphonies, many of them written while he held the backbreaking post of director to the Vienna Court Opera, are widely considered to be the finest works of the late Austro-German symphonic tradition. In four of his symphonies, Mahler attempted a synthesis of song and symphonic form.

Mahler was also one of the major conductors of his time. His meteoric rise from provincial origins to the pre-eminent conducting post in Austria ended in 1907 when anti-Semitic forced him to resign his post in Vienna. Undaunted, he travelled to New York to became chief conductor at the Metropolitan Opera, returning to Europe to give the legendary 1910 performance of his Eighth 'Symphony of a Thousand' in Munich. He died the following year, having lived a life of intense over-activity.

Jules Massenet (1843–1912) was born to a wealthy French family. He showed exceptional musical gifts and was admitted to the Paris Conservatoire at the age of 11. In 1863, with the support of Berlioz, he won the famous Prix de Rome. In 1870 he served, alongside his friend Bizet, in the national guard during the Franco-Prussian War.

Massenet's life was divided between his responsibilities as professor at the Paris Conservatoire (where his influence as a teacher was considerable) and his brilliant career as an opera composer. His greatest successes, *Manon*, *Thaïs* and *Werther* skilfully integrate religious-erotic conflict in a warm, colourfully melodic style.

Hubert Parry (1848–1918) was an English composer of outstanding intellectual powers. He read history and law at Oxford while studying music privately in his spare time. He was a progressive thinker and a keen advocate of Charles Darwin's evolutionary theory. For a period, he was a Lloyd's underwriter but abandoned it for a career in music.

Parry's output includes five impressive symphonies and three biblical oratorios, but his most famous works are his magnificent church anthems, *Blest Pair of Sirens* and *I was Glad* (originally composed for the coronation of Edward VII). His unison setting of *Jerusalem* has become an unofficial English national anthem.

Nikolay Rimsky-Korsakov (1844–1908) was born into a noble Russian family and started his musical education while serving as a naval officer. He soon became a member of The Five, a hugely influential group of Russian nationalist composers including Mussorgsky, Borodin and Balakirev who gave him informal tuition. During this period, Rimsky-Korsakov wrote his orchestral pieces *Antar*, establishing his reputation as a major talent.

In 1871 Rimsky-Korsakov became a professor at the St Petersburg Conservatory. During this period, he perfected his own compositional technique and wrote his brilliant orchestration treatise and the orchestral showpiece, *Sheherazade*. Glazunov and Stravinsky were among his illustrious students. During his later career he produced a remarkable quantity of spectacular operas including *Sadko* (1897) and *The Golden Cockerel* (1907).

Erik Satie (1866–1925) was a French composer of remarkable originality and eccentricity. He studied at the Paris Conservatoire where he was describes as 'gifted but indolent'. He won no awards. Among his earliest pieces were the *Gymnopédies* (1888) and *Gnossiennes* (1890) whose languid beauty and originality influenced his friend Debussy.

Satie earned his living as a café pianist in Montmartre before retiring in 1898 to a life of self-imposed poverty. Meanwhile, he composed a number of pieces with bizarre titles like *Three Pieces in the form of a Pear*. In later years, Satie's music was championed by Ravel and Jean Cocteau. The latter collaborated with Satie on a ballet, *Parade* (1917) which included typewriters and other surreal instruments in the score.

Alexander Skryabin (1872–1915) was a composer with mystical tendencies. As a child, his ear was so good that he could replicate on the piano any music he heard, and by the age of 11 he was already a virtuoso pianist. His early piano music was strongly influenced by Chopin.

His later music developed in complex and surprising ways. He began to devise his own kind of 'mystical' harmony, free from the constraints of traditional tonality. His symphonies and orchestral pieces became increasingly ambitious in scale and more and more exotic in harmony and sound. His late masterpieces, *Poem of Ecstasy* and *Prometheus, the Poem of Fire* are mysterious and exciting. In later years, Skryabin's mysticism went to his head and he started to speak of himself in messianic terms. He died suddenly in 1915.

Johann Strauss II (1825–1899) was the son of Johann Strauss I, the most successful waltz composer of his generation. His father attempted to discourage Johann's musical talents but the boy responded by eventually setting up his own orchestra. It became a successful rival to his father's!

Strauss surpassed his father with his genius for inspired and elegant melodies, richly harmonised and beautifully orchestrated. With his touring orchestra, Strauss became an international celebrity. His waltzes are magnificent but probably his greatest achievement was his flawless operetta, *Die Fledermaus*.

Pyotr Ilyich Tchaikovsky (1840–1893) initially studied law at the St Petersburg School of Jurisprudence but rapidly discovered his talent for composition when he started taking lessons from Anton Rubenstein. Encouraged by Balakirev he composed his first masterpiece, the fantasy overture *Romeo and Juliet*.

Thereafter, an extraordinary sequence of masterpieces flowed from his pen, including six symphonies, two piano concertos, a violin concerto, several operas and the three magnificent ballets: *Swan Lake, Sleeping Beauty* and *The Nutcracker*. Tchaikovsky's music is remarkable for its vivid emotionality as much as for its stylistic elegance and melodic grace. He died nine days after completing his swan song, the *Pathétique* Symphony; a work of such heartfelt intensity that many believe Tchaikovsky consciously composed it as his own requiem.

Giuseppe Verdi (1813–1901) was the son of an innkeeper in rural Parma. His musical talent was first noticed by a local merchant who subsequently sponsored Verdi's private music lessons in Milan. His first opera, *Oberto* (1839) was a relative success but it was not until the first performance of *Nabucco* at La Scala, Milan in 1842 that Verdi became an Italian national hero. Not content to repeat the formula, Verdi went on to even greater achievements in *Macbeth* (1847) and *Rigoletto* (1848).

His middle-period operas, *Il Travatore* (1852) and *La Traviata* (1853) helped to consolidate Verdi's position as the most original Italian opera composer of his time, a supremely imaginative musical dramatist and a melodic genius. After the grand operas, *Don Carlos* (1867) and *Aïda* (1873) Verdi took a break of 15 years before he returned to composing stage works. During this period, he wrote his famous Requiem and revised his earlier masterpiece *Simon Boccanegra* before finally undertaking his greatest achievements, the final operas *Otello* (1887) and the comic opera *Falstaff* (1893).

Hungarian Dance
(in G minor)

Composed by Johannes Brahms

Allegretto
(from Symphony No.3 in F)

Composed by Johannes Brahms

12

Waltz, Op.39, No.15

Composed by Johannes Brahms

Wiegenlied
(Cradle Song/Lullaby)

Composed by Johannes Brahms

dim. e rall. al fine

Violin Concerto
(Slow movement)

Composed by Max Bruch
Arranged by Jerry Lanning

23

Locus Iste

Composed by Anton Bruckner

Arranged by Andrew Skirrow

Allegro moderato

Démand Et Reponse

Composed by Samuel Coleridge-Taylor

Arabesque No.1

Composed by Claude Debussy

Tempo rubato
(un peu moins vite)

Clair De Lune
(from Suite Bergamasque)

Composed by Claude Debussy

Andante très expressif

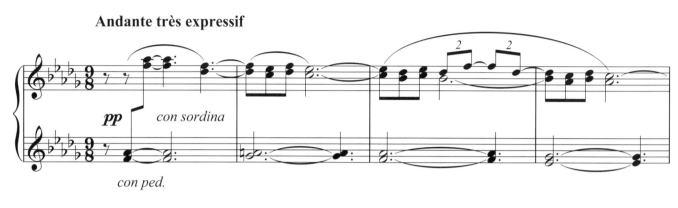

Tempo rubato

En animant

Tempo I

pp *morendo jusqu'à la fin*

Humoresque, Op.101, No.7

Composed by Antonin Dvořák

Largo
(from The New World Symphony)

Composed by Antonin Dvořák

Largo ♩ = 48

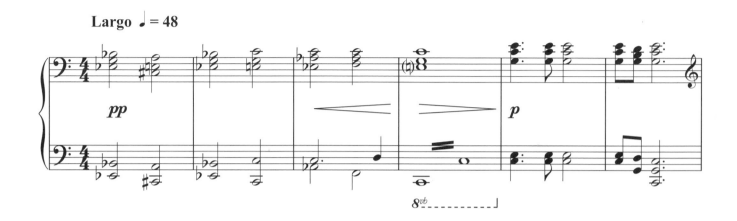

Serenade For Strings in E Minor

(1st movement: Moderato)

Composed by Antonin Dvořák

Arranged by Jerry Lanning

Tango
(Op.165 No.2)

Composed by Isaac Albéniz

Chanson De Matin

Composed by Edward Elgar

Salut D'Amour

Composed by Edward Elgar

Agnus Dei
(from Requiem)

Composed by Gabriel Fauré

Après Un Rêve

Composed by Gabriel Fauré

Andantino

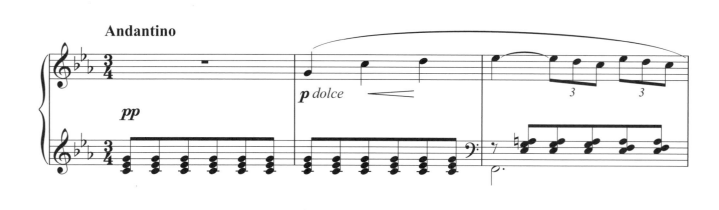

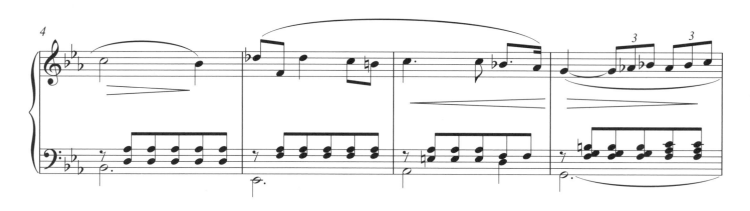

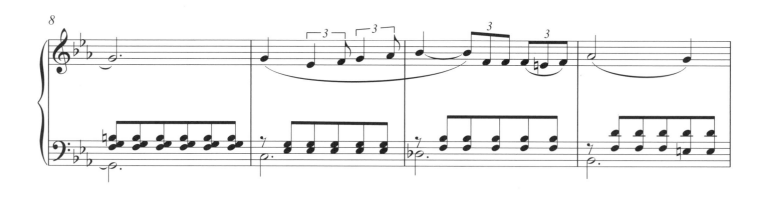

In Paradisum

(from Requiem)

Composed by Gabriel Fauré
Arranged by Quentin Thomas

Song Without Words
(Op. 17, No. 3)

Composed by Gabriel Fauré

Andante moderato ♩ = 76

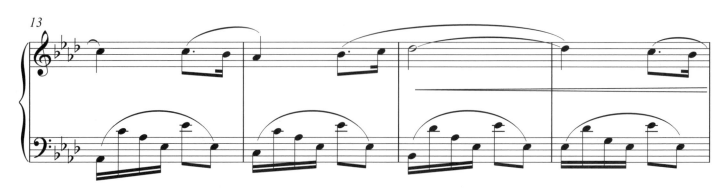

Pavane

Composed by Gabriel Fauré

Andante molto moderato

Norwegian Dance
(Op.35, No.2)

Composed by Edvard Grieg

Anitra's Dance
(from Peer Gynt)

Composed by Edvard Grieg

Tempo di Mazurka (♩ = 160)

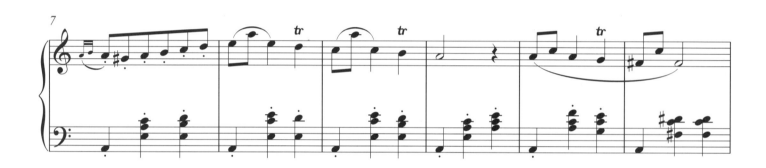

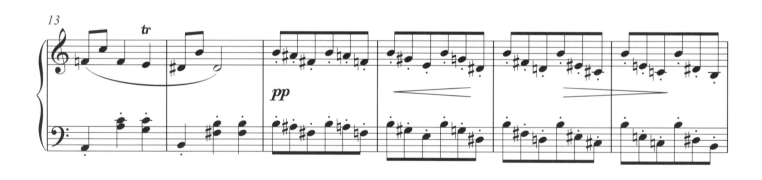

Notturno
(Op.54, No.4)

Composed by Edvard Grieg

Piano Concerto in A minor
(Opening)

Composed by Edvard Grieg
Arranged by Jerry Lanning

Maple Leaf Rag

Composed by Scott Joplin

Tempo di marcia

The Entertainer

Composed by Scott Joplin

(repeat R.H. 8va. higher)

Gymnopédie No. 1

Composed by Erik Satie

Lent et douloureux

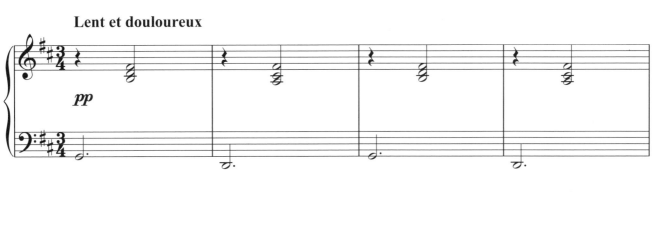

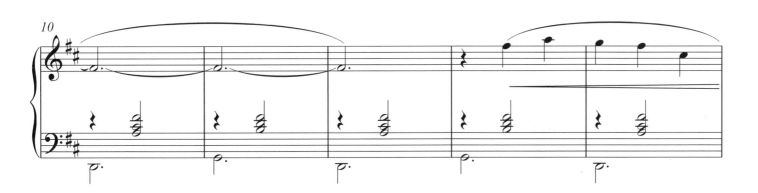

To A Wild Rose

Composed by Edward MacDowell

Adagietto
(from Symphony No. 5)

Composed by Gustav Mahler

Very slow

Meditation

(from Thaïs)

Composed by Jules Massenet

rall.   a tempo

Jerusalem

Composed by C. Hubert H. Parry

Arranged by Andrew Skirrow

The Young Prince and Young Princess
(from Sheherazade)

Composed by Nikolai Rimsky-Korsakov

Prelude

(Op.11, No.4)

Composed by Alexander Scriabin

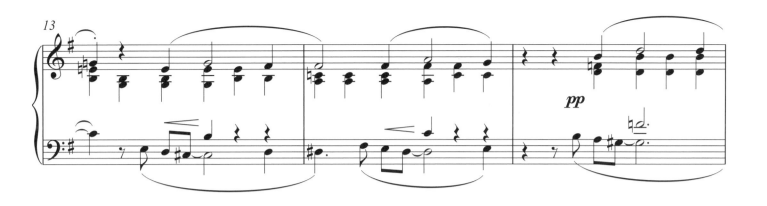

Accelerations Waltz
(Op.234)

Composed by Johann Strauss II

125

Emperor Waltz

Composed by Johann Strauss II

Tempo di Valse (♩ = 132)

Waltz: Voices Of Spring

Composed by Johann Strauss II

Tempo di valse (♩. = 64)

Chinese Dance
(from The Nutcracker)

Composed by Peter Ilych Tchaikovsky

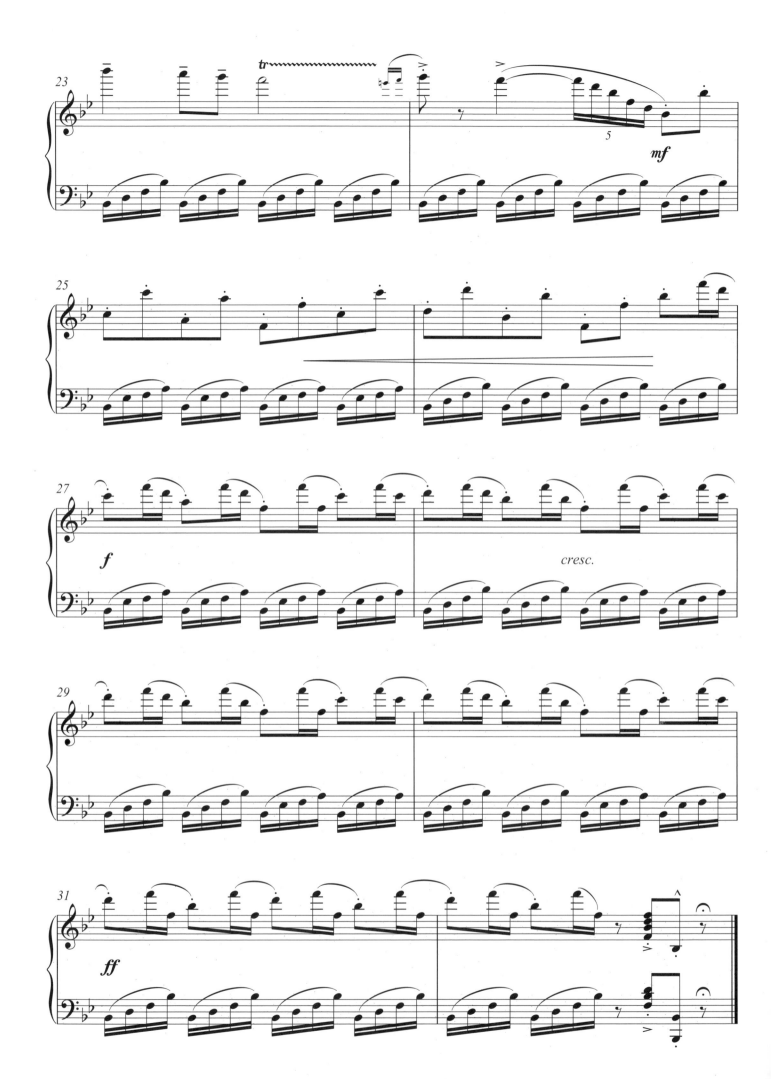

138

Love Theme

(from Romeo and Juliet)

Composed by Peter Ilych Tchaikovsky

Allegro giusto (♩ = 60)

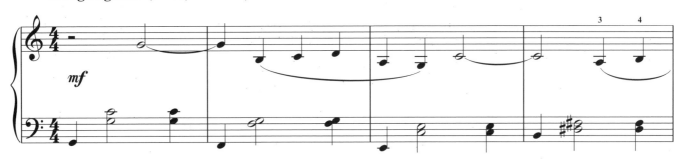

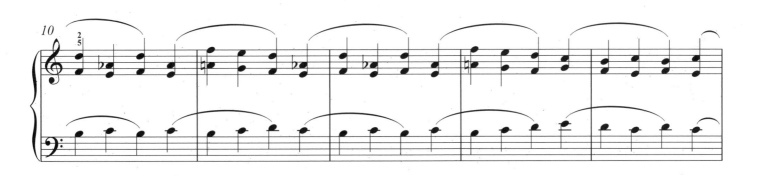

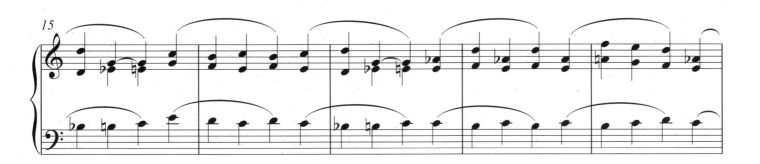

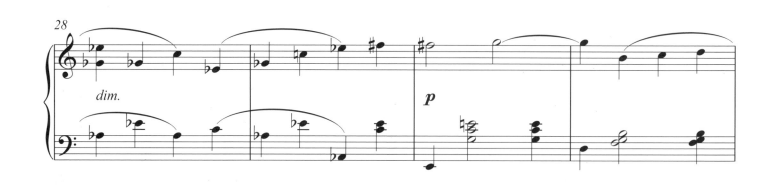

Piano Concerto, No. 1

(1st movement: Allegro)

Composed by Peter Ilych Tchaikovsky

Slavonic March

(Op.31, 1st section)

Composed by Peter Ilych Tchaikovsky

Allegro moderato

Swan Lake
(Scene from Act II)

Composed by Peter Ilych Tchaikovsky

stringendo   più mosso

Waltz Of The Flowers
(from The Nutcracker)

Composed by Peter Ilych Tchaikovsky

Very freely and held back

a tempo di valse moderato

Dies Irae
(from Requiem)

Composed by Giuseppe Verdi

Allegro agitato ($\lsd = 80$)

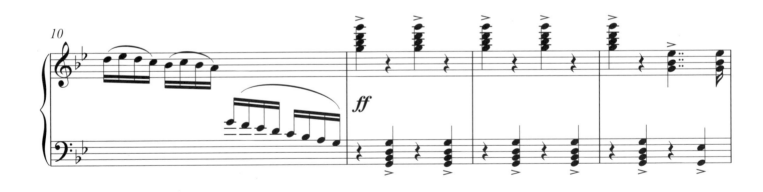